How To Change Someone's Mind

by Mike Slater

Printed in the United States of America

First Printing, 2017

ISBN 978-1973725749

TABLE OF CONTENTS

To my wife, for your constant support.

To my eight month old son. May we all talk
differently to each other by the time you can talk.

1. How to Change Minds

Every Saturday morning, my fellow college tour guides and I would stand up on a ledge and give a brief introduction of ourselves to about 100 eager high school students and parents. I would say, "My name is Mike. I'm on the swim team. I write for the college newspaper and I am the token conservative on campus." The tour guides would split up and people would then choose which tour guide they wanted for the next ninety minutes.

After a few weeks I asked the other tour guides why there were so many people from Texas taking the tours. They said they hadn't met a single person from Texas. It turns out, all the Texans, and conservatives, just chose to take my tour.

Invariably, I'd be asked what it's like to be a conservative at Yale, a university lately known for being a bastion of liberalism. I would say, "I love it. You talk with people you disagree with and one of two things happen: either you strengthen your opinion, or you change your mind. Both are good things."

That was ten years ago. I've recently realized, I haven't changed my mind on anything since…well, maybe since college. Is this because I have finally figured out all the answers? I doubt it.

When was the last time you changed your mind about anything significant? Let's start with politics. Have you in the last ten years changed your mind on a specific political issue? If your answer is no, I would guess you are not alone. It is so easy to join a team, dig in your heels, only listen to people you agree with and never question anything. Even the thought of changing your mind might make you feel like you are betraying a friend.

Moreover, when was the last time you changed someone else's mind? Have you convinced a boss, co-worker, friend, spouse or neighbor to see something your way? Have you ever persuaded a family member to change their vote over the Thanksgiving dinner table? Have you managed to influence someone's view via an online comment section or twitter reply? I have not.

Until I learned how.

David figured it out. He reached out to Megan online. They didn't know each other, but he always remained friendly. A few months later, David finally met Megan in person. He brought her a gift: a Middle Eastern dessert from his home town of Jerusalem. There was nothing particularly odd about this interaction; other than the fact that, at the time, Megan was holding a giant sign that read "God Hates Jews."

Megan was a member of the Westboro Baptist Church, a hate-filled cult that is known for protesting military funerals and saying horrible things against homosexuals and Jews.

Megan had argued with countless people on the internet. She would tell everyone why she was right and why they were wrong, why she was going to heaven and you were going to hell. And each time people would attack her right back. No one on either side ever changed their mind. But the interactions with David were different. His approach: "I wanted to be really nice so that [Megan] would have a hard time hating me."

Remarkably, this approach softened her heart. Over time, Megan and her sister decided to leave their "church," a decision that meant she would never see her family again. Where did she go? She reached out to David. She ended up sleeping on a couch in the home of his Hasidic Rabbi. Just three years earlier, Megan was protesting outside this man's synagogue with a sign that read "Your rabbi is a whore." Now she sought shelter in his home and joined his wife and four kids around their dinner table.

Megan said, "They treated [my sister and me] like family. They held nothing against us, and I was astonished."[1]

Megan now speaks out against bigotry and hatred. At one event, sponsored by the Times of Israel, Megan said, "David told me about *tikkun olam,* the Jewish teaching that you could do something to repair the world. [Westboro Baptist Church] literally had a website, 'The World is Doomed,' but this idea that we could fix what we broke, this really gave me hope in a time where there wasn't a lot of that."[2]

I want more interactions like David and Megan's in my life and in this nation. I want my eight month old son to live in a country where people talk differently to each other than we do now. Call me a hopeless romantic, but I'm guessing you want this, too. Otherwise you wouldn't be reading this.

This book is about how to change someone's heart and mind.

The goal is to change how we talk to each other.

If these truths can be used to rescue a stranger from a cult, they can be helpful when talking politics and religion with a co-worker, neighbor, or family member with polar opposite views.

I have been the host of a political talk radio show for ten years. On talk radio, there's a lot of preaching to the choir. I'm good at that. There are also opportunities to change a person's mind on a given topic. I've done a pretty terrible job at that for most of these ten years.

After every show I get e-mails from people saying, "What a great show! I've never heard that argument before! That's such a great point!" But I rarely receive an e-mail that says, "You've changed my mind."

I consider this a failure. But it has given me extra insight into what it takes to do the seemingly impossible.

2. What This Book is Not

Conservative writer Ben Shapiro wrote a book a few years ago, *How to Debate Leftists and Destroy Them: 11 Rules for Winning the Argument.* On the progressive side, Hillary Clinton's campaign published a post on her campaign website, "How to win a Thanksgiving debate with Republicans."[3]

This book is *not* about how to win an argument. Do you want to know how to win an argument? Speak more confidently than the other guy. You can be totally wrong and have completely made up facts, but whoever is more aggressive, louder and sounds more certain "wins." (If you host a radio show, you can also hang up on a caller. That's an easy path to victory!)

This book will not help you be more aggressive, louder or more confident sounding. Actually, quite the opposite. I did those things for ten years. It doesn't work and it is painfully unfulfilling. Have you ever had a family dinner end with silverware being thrown and someone marching away from the table? What good does that do? Sure, someone "won", but someone else lost, and that person will never end up agreeing with you. They'll just be mad at you. And this opinion you have, which presumably is so important that you want everyone else to have it, too? Now there's one less person who will ever have it.

You can win the argument, but did you really win?

This book will also not help you win Facebook or Twitter arguments. Those are pointless. Don't partake. Don't engage. Don't waste your time. Unless, like David and Megan's experience, your online interaction is planting a seed which later leads to a more personal interaction (which we'll talk about in the Rules Section coming up).

This book won't help you combat online trolls. As my Tennessee friends say, "Don't wrestle with pigs. You get muddy and the pigs love it."

Finally, this book is not just about politics. Because I have a political job, most of my experience is in that realm, but these insights can be applied anywhere about any topic. I'm sure you've heard the advice, "Two things you should never talk about: religion or politics." And we wonder why these topics are so divisive. It is not because we talk about them too much. It's because we don't talk about them enough! Or, more precisely, we don't talk about them the right way.

So what is the right way? Let's start off with some foundational truths.

3. Beat It Down

Ben Franklin used to be very prideful.

When he was seventeen, he left Boston for Philadelphia. Seven months later, he returned to his hometown, ready to show everyone how much money he was making. He especially wanted to show off to Cotton Mather, a wealthy and respected man in town.

He met Mather in a hallway and as they walked towards the exit, Franklin started unloading about how successful he was. Mather responded, "Stoop!"

Franklin was so into himself, he kept bragging and ran his head into a low ceiling beam.

Mather's response, without skipping a beat, "Stoop, young man, stoop - as you go through this world - and you'll miss many hard thumps."[4]

It wasn't until Franklin received this letter from a friend when it really hit him:

> Ben, you are impossible. Your opinions have a slap in them for everyone who differs with

you. They have become so offensive that no-body cares for them. Your friends find they enjoy themselves better when you are not around. You know so much that no man can tell you anything. Indeed, no man is going to try, for the effort would lead only to discomfort and hard work. So you are not likely ever to know any more than you do now, which is very little.

Be honest. Could anyone describe you that way?

That is a stinging rebuke from a friend and it had to hurt. Fortunately for everyone, Franklin responded with life-saving humility. He wrote about it to his nephew:

> A Quaker friend having kindly informed me that I was generally thought proud; that my pride showed itself frequently in conversation; that I was not content with being in the right when discussing any point, but was overbearing, and rather insolent [arrogant], of which he convinced me by mentioning several instances; I determined endeavoring to cure myself, if I could, of this vice or folly among the rest, and I

added Humility to my list, giving an extensive meaning to the word.[5]

Franklin decided to no longer contradict or forcibly "show [the] absurdity" in another person's argument. He offered his opinions with less emphatic phrases and instead used, "it so appears to me at present", or "in certain cases [your] opinion would be right, but in the present case there seems to me some difference."

Franklin engaged in more pleasant (and less combative) conversation. Over time, as this became natural to him, Franklin realized how persuasive and influential he became:

> To this habit I think it principally owing that I had early so much weight with my fellow citizens when I proposed new institutions, or alterations in the old, and so much influence in public councils when I became a member...

Here, Franklin gives his nephew, and us, important advice as we try to change other people's minds: we must tame our pride:

In reality, there is, perhaps, no one of our natural passions so hard to subdue as pride. Disguise it, struggle with it, beat it down, stifle it, mortify it as much as one pleases...

This new, humbled Ben Franklin would have been a terrible guest on a cable news debate show. For some reason, we feel we need to talk to each other as though we are all TV pundits. We are convinced that we need to show the absurdity of the other person's opinion. We think we need to shut them down as quickly as possible!

Wouldn't we all be better off if we conversed like Ben?

We tend to see humility as weakness. But it is pride that kills conversations and weakens our influence. Beat it down.

4. You Can't Make Them Drink

- Fact 1: It is much easier to change someone's mind if they *want* their mind to be changed.

- Fact 2: Almost no one ever wants their mind to be changed.

Let that sink in for a second. It's hard to accept because you're thinking, "Why wouldn't someone want to know the truth? They're wrong, I'm right. Of course they want to hear what I have to say!"

No they don't.

Why don't they want to 'know the truth?'

We associate the strength of our opinions with our own self-worth. If we are in a debate with someone and they make a really good point on an issue, deep down in our subconscious, we say to ourselves, "Darn it. He's on to something. But if I change my mind, I have to admit I'm wrong. And if I'm wrong, it means I'm stupid. And I don't want to be stupid. So, I won't admit I'm wrong."

This happens as fast as it takes to go from zero to defensive: a split-second. We will do anything to protect our egos.

This is why it might feel like someone is actively looking for reasons not to agree with you. They probably are. What they are really doing is looking for reasons to agree with themselves.

When we are confronted with new information, we subconsciously ask ourselves one of two questions...

5. "Must I?" vs "Can I?"

Have you ever shared a documented fact with someone and they just refuse to believe it? This person, who is otherwise a reasonable and sensible person, has just turned into a brick wall. You're thinking, "Gosh, if they would just accept this one fact, then they would definitely change their mind! Why won't they just accept it?!"

Cornell University psychologist Tom Gilovich has found that if someone does not want to believe something, they ask themselves, "Must I believe this?" And they look for one reason why they don't have to.[6]

They do this because they want to avoid admitting they are wrong. It looks like the person isn't listening to you— because they're not. It feels like they don't want to believe you — because they don't. They are actively searching for a reason not to believe you.

Scientists asked women to read a fake study about a link between caffeine consumption and breast cancer. Women who are heavy coffee drinkers found more flaws in the study than women who don't drink coffee. The coffee drinkers looked for reasons not to believe it.[7]

On the other hand, have you ever been amazed at how quickly someone will believe a preposterous statement?

This person, who is otherwise a reasonable and sensible person, has just turned into a gullible fool. You're thinking, "How could they believe something so stupid and obviously untrue!"

It's because, if someone is inclined to believe something, instead of asking, "Must I believe it?" they ask themselves, "Can I believe it?" And they look for one reason why they can. Really, what they are asking is, "Can I agree with what I already think is true?" As often as possible, they will respond, "Yes!"

Let's start with a hypothetical example. Two people see a newspaper headline, "UFO Spotted by Local Resident." The person who believes in aliens asks themselves, "Can I believe this?" And they look for one reason why they can. Their reason can be as simple as, "Why would the newspaper publish this if it wasn't true!"

The person who does not believe in aliens asks themselves, "Must I believe this?" And they look for one reason why they don't have to. They will reason something like, "Why didn't more than just that one person see the UFO? Therefore, this story is false."

Each person is looking to validate their previously held beliefs.

Global warming is another good example. If someone is inclined to believe in man-made global warming, they ask themselves, "Can I believe this?" Al Gore shows a picture of a polar bear seemingly trapped on an iceberg and they're convinced it is true.

If someone is inclined not to believe in man-made global warming, they ask themselves, "Must I believe this?" They see it's snowing somewhere in the world and they're convinced it's all a lie.

We reject information that might prove us wrong because we don't like to admit we are wrong. That feels bad. We are quick to let in information that proves we are already right because we like to affirm we are right. That feels good. This turns us into either brick walls or gullible fools.

After we form an opinion, we go to great lengths to polish and perfect that opinion for the rest of our lives.

This means you cannot just jump right into changing someone's mind. It's a process. The first goal is NOT to change someone's mind; it is to get someone to want to change their mind. We will get to that later.

First we need to know how we form opinions.

6. How Do People Form Opinions?

Answer: Instantly.

I am not exaggerating. We form opinions in a heartbeat.

Princeton University researchers wanted to learn how quickly we make judgments of other people. They flashed sixty-six faces on a screen for either .1 second, .5 second or a full second. After each face flashed on the screen and then disappeared, people marked how trustworthy they believe that person is and how confident they were of their judgment.

Professor Alex Todorov explained, "What we found was that, if given more time, people's fundamental judgment about faces did not change. Observers simply became more confident in their judgments as the duration lengthened."[8]

This means the observer came to an initial judgment in .1 second, and then, as time went on (another .9 seconds), they spent that time convincing themselves how right they were.

In another study conducted in 2007, Professor Todorov showed subjects two faces of people they had never seen before. He asked them to make a split-second gut reaction, based only on their faces, of who appeared more competent. What the subjects didn't realize was that these were the faces of people who ran for US Senate in the 2006 election.

When asked who looked more competent, people ended up picking the winning candidate 70% of the time. Todorov: "This means that, with a quick look at two photos, you have a great chance of predicting who will win. Voters are not that rational, after all."[9]

The suggestion is, and I believe it is true, that most people make up their mind on who they are voting for instantly. The rest of the campaign, therefore, is an expensive exercise of rationalization.

That's not all. People will even defend "decisions" they never actually made. Researchers showed the subject two pictures of two different people and asked them to choose who is more attractive: person A or person B.

If the subject chose person A, the researchers distracted them for a split second and *switched the pictures*. They then asked the subject why they thought person A was more attractive (even though, now, they're looking at person B).

Only 25% of the time would people say, "Wait a second, I actually chose the other person." The other 75% of the time, the subjects went on to explain why they chose this person, even though they actually chose the other person! People will go to great lengths to justify their initial opinions and prove themselves right.[10]

But why do we form opinions so quickly? Daniel Goleman coined the term "amygdala hijack."[11] The amygdala is the part of the brain that is in charge of emotional reactions. When the brain gets a stimulus, the amygdala processes information faster than the reasoning part of the brain. This is our natural fight-or-flight response, and it can't be turned off. That is a good thing...most of the time.[12]

The problem is, we do the same thing when it comes to forming opinions; from someone's attractiveness and trustworthiness, to choosing a candidate for president.

And then our ego prevents us from ever questioning that conclusion again.

7. Built-Up Defenses

We are naturally very defensive. This is a good thing. That amygdala we just referenced helps us react to physical threats quickly. If a baseball comes flying towards your head, the amygdala reacts faster than the rational part of your brain. This is good because you don't need to react rationally in the first .01 seconds. You just need to duck.

The problem is, we react to people challenging our opinions the same way we might react to a flying projectile coming towards our face.

To protect ourselves from people challenging our opinions and core beliefs, we build up a massive, protective wall.

Your goal, if you want to change someone's mind, is not to remove their wall yourself. Your goal is to have the other person dismantle their wall *themselves*, brick by brick.

If you want to "win an argument," then you should launch cannon balls into their defenses. If you want to change someone's mind, then you need to get them to remove their own wall. See the difference?

One piece of advice that Ben Shapiro gives in his book *How to Debate Leftists and Destroy Them*, is, "Don't take the punch first. Hit first. Hit hard. Hit where it counts."[13] Fine advice if you want to win the argument. Not good advice if you want to change their minds.

Take a step back. What does it feel like to have your own wall attacked?

Matthew Inman, the writer of the webcomic The Oatmeal," gives this example:

We all know that George Washington had wooden teeth. Have you heard that before? It's not true.

In 2005, the National Museum of Dentistry in Baltimore scanned a pair of his dentures and found they were made of gold, lead, hippopotamus ivory, horse and donkey teeth.[14]

Now that I've told you that fact, how do you feel? Check your emotional gauge. You probably feel fine. That's an interesting fact you may not have known.

The thing is, George Washington had another set of false teeth. This set was made from the teeth of slaves.

Now how do you feel?

Probably a bit more heated. You probably accepted my first fact about Washington's teeth with no problem, but now you don't believe the second fact, or you're mad at me because you think I'm attacking the father of our country.

Why do we react differently to the second fact? Because you probably had a worldview that George Washington was a hero and a patriot. I presented negative information about him that challenged one of your core beliefs. That's what it feels like to have your opinions and defensive wall attacked. It makes you want to attack back and build an even stronger defensive wall.

So how do you get someone to take their guard down?

WARNING: This might be the most important part of the secret. But before I tell you, let me say that I realize you might be annoyed. This is the part of the book when you will probably stop reading. I have always wanted so desperately for the secret to be something I can do, or a weapon with which I can arm myself. I want to build up my arguing arsenal and, with this one secret, be able to magically change people's minds, all without changing anything about myself!

If that is you, you will be disappointed.

But if you think that what you believe is so vitally important, and you really want to *actually* change people's minds and have them agree with you, consider this:

You can only change someone's mind if you are willing to change yours.

"Hold on, Slater. I thought this book was about how to change someone *else's* mind! I don't want to change my mind. I don't *need* to change my mind. I'm the one who is right!"

I know you are, but instead of taking your confidence in your opinion and building a giant wall around it, be vulnerable yourself. Take your wall down. Just like Ben Franklin's pride, beat it down. Terrifying though it may seem, be willing to let your opinion be challenged without any defenses. This is the only way someone will ever be willing to let *their* opinion be challenged.

Let me be clear: this does not mean you have to change your mind. It just means you have to be *willing* to change it.

Thomas Jefferson wrote this note to his nephew. He was specifically talking about religion, but it's true for everything:

Your reason is now mature enough to examine [religion]. In the first place, divest yourself of all bias...Fix reason firmly in her seat, and call to her tribunal every fact, every opinion. Question with boldness even the existence of a God; because, if there be one, he must more approve of the homage of reason, than that of blind-folded fear.[15]

Jefferson did not say, "Nephew, never question your beliefs and attack as many people as possible for theirs." He never gave advice on how to crush his opponents.

Like Jefferson's nephew, I think you are mature enough to examine your opinions, and to have them examined by someone else. If you think you are right about something, be confident enough to be questioned boldly. Don't hold on to your opinion in fear that it might be shattered. If it is worthy, it will withstand the honest inquiry. If not, then maybe it is time to see things differently. In reality, if you push aside your pride, you have nothing to lose and everything to gain.

Be willing to have your mind changed.

8. Rules of Mind Changing

Rule 1: Build respect.

No one will be vulnerable in front of you or agree with you if they don't respect you. How do you earn respect? Give respect.

Jen is a twenty-nine year old political liberal. Her dad is conservative. They constantly fight about politics. It never goes well. The last time they tried to have a discussion, Jen ended it with, "I can't even talk to you, dad!"

Can you relate?

During the 2016 election, the non-profit organization StoryCorps recorded one of their conversations. Dad and daughter started out yelling at each other, "You said this! You think that!" but then, one statement from dad completely changed the tone of the conversation. It changed the mood of the room. You could feel it. First, they are angry and yelling at each other:

> **Dad**: I get miffed when you say you can't talk to me. But if you're going to get so angry and flip out about it, then I'd rather you didn't talk to me.

Jen: See this is what drives me crazy though! I am not the only one yelling in our conversations.

Dad: But I ask questions. 'What do you think about this? What do you think about that?" It's me trying to glean information from someone who is significantly more educated than I am and whose opinions I trust.

This is when everything changes. You can hear it in Jen's voice. She lets her guard down completely.

Jen: I am really surprised to hear you say that. I had no idea that you were genuinely interested in what I had to say. I thought that you wanted to tell me how I was wrong and to make a joke about how I was silly.

Dad: I would never feel that way about you. I have nothing but respect for you. I don't agree with you all the time, but that's okay."[16]

From that point forward, it was like two different people were talking to each other. Two people who respected each other, even if they disagreed.

Having respect for someone has to be more than a strategy. People can sense your authenticity, or lack thereof. People are perceptive. They can tell if, deep down, you have an ulterior motive or agenda. If they catch wind of it, the trust is eroded. They won't feel safe. They will never take their walls down. Respect them. And mean it.

Rule 2: Go one on one.

It is extremely difficult to change someone's mind around a group of people. It's hard enough to admit we are wrong to ourselves. No one likes to admit they're wrong around other people.

A study called the Asch Conformity Experiment had eight people sit around a table. Seven of the people were actors. They were in on the experiment. Only one person was actually being observed.

Psychologist Solomon Asch showed everyone a drawing of a line, called the reference line. Then he showed everyone three lines of varying lengths: lines A, B, and C. He then asked everyone which line was the same length as the reference line. The answer was obviously C. But the actors, as they answered going around the table, all answered A on purpose. A was clearly the wrong answer.

A
B
C

They did this twelve times; 75% of the people being observed followed the group opinion and gave the obviously wrong answer at least once.[17]

We are social creatures. We want to be liked. Group conformity — the peer pressure to go along with the group (even when we know the group is wrong) — is a powerful force. It is best not to work against it. If you want to change someone's mind, a one-on-one, in-person conversation avoids this obstacle.

Rule 3: Gauge the temperature.

A Pyrrhic victory is when you achieve your goal, but at too great a cost.

It is named after King Pyrrhus in Greece. He was determined in 281 BC to carve out his own massive empire in Europe, starting with Italy.

In his first battle with the Romans, the Romans were winning. But King Pyrrhus had a secret weapon: elephants. The Romans had never seen elephants used in battle before. They were terrified and retreated. Pyrrhus won the battle, but he took heavy losses.

Two years later, in their second battle, Pyrrhus won again, but almost all of his generals were killed and he himself was badly wounded. Pyrrhus was congratulated for his victories, yet he responded, "If we defeat the Romans in one more such battle, we shall be totally ruined."[18]

He was already ruined. His army never recovered. His Italian campaign was over.

You, unlike King Pyrrhus, need to be able to know when to move forward and when to fall back. You must constantly gauge the emotional temperature of the conversation. If it gets too hot, you may "win" the debate, but at too great a cost.

Watch your tone of voice and body language. Most of communication is not what you say, it is how you say it. Always stay calm and keep your body relaxed. If your tone becomes aggressive or assertive, then their defenses will go up.

If you sense a *hint* of negative emotion from the other person, don't push it. Their guard is up. Pull back a bit. See if the temperature goes back down. If it doesn't go back down, that's okay. It might not be happening today. Talk about something else. Don't force it.

Sun Tzu said in The Art of War, "When the weapons have grown dull and spirits depressed…even if you have wise generals you cannot make things turn out well in the end."[19] When it comes to communicating with someone, when anger has increased and our patience is depressed, even if you have the wisest arguments, it is very hard to make things turn out well in the end.

Know when it's getting too hot.

Rule 4: Play the long game.

Don't feel like the fate of the world depends on you changing this person's mind right here, on the spot. It doesn't. You are not MacGyver diffusing a bomb in thirty seconds. You have time. And it won't happen with the perfect, golden one-liner, so don't worry about trying to find the killshot. It may take many conversations over a long period of time to change someone's mind. Be patient.

When David talked to Westboro Baptist Church member Megan online, he knew there wasn't going to be a magic tweet that would immediately transform her heart.

One day, David asked her a question she could not answer. She internally struggled with that question for *two years* before she finally realized she didn't have a good answer. It takes time to change minds.

No matter how handsome or brilliant you are, you will never get the person to fall on their knees, thanking you for helping them see the light. Get rid of that expectation. Relax and build the relationship. Take some pressure off yourself.

Instead, think about it as planting seeds. It will take time for them to grow. Your desperation to get them to see it your way will only make *them* desperate *not* to see it your way.

Rule 5: Avoid the "Butwhatabout" pitfall.

Pick *one* topic and stick with it. Don't let them change the topic. If people feel trapped or desperate, they will say what amounts to, "Oh ya, but what about *this* completely unrelated thing I'm bringing up because it feels like I'm losing this argument."

I call this the "Butwhatabout" argument. If you are talking about the 2nd Amendment, the other person, if they feel desperate and cornered, will say, "Oh ya, butwhatabout global warming! Butwhatabout taxes! Butwhatabout, whatabout, whatabout!"

If you bring up something more relational, the person might feel cornered and say, "Oh ya?! Butwhatabout that one time when you...!"

When they do this, nicely bring them back to the topic at hand: "We can address that in a second, but let's finish this conversation first." If they won't stay on topic, they don't want their mind changed. That's okay. Move on for now.

There's a sixth rule, The Costanza Rule. We will get to that one later.

9. The Opinion Box

We are selfish people. We assume that everyone cares about our opinion. The truth is, almost no one cares.

Do you want to know a trick to getting the other person to respect you and open up to you? Before you tell them what you think about a topic, ask them what they think.

Dale Carnegie wrote in *How to Win Friends and Influence People*, "A person's name is to that person the sweetest and most important sound in any language."

Carnegie tells the story of Sid Levy who called on a customer named Nicodemus Papadoulos. He told people to call him "Nick," but Levy went the extra mile:

> I made a special effort to say his name over several times to myself before I made my call. When I greeted him by his full name: 'Good afternoon, Mr. Nicodemus Papadoulos,' he was shocked. For what seemed like several minutes there was no reply from him at all. Finally, he said with tears rolling down his cheeks, 'Mr. Levy, in all the fifteen years I have been in this

country, nobody has ever made the effort to call me by my right name.'"[20]

The person whose mind you are trying to change, I wonder if, in all their life, anyone has ever asked them their opinion on something. If there is anything sweeter than the sound of their name, it is someone caring enough to actually ask their opinion.

So ask questions. Be genuinely curious. And keep asking more questions.

The image I have is that everyone has a box full of opinions. You may want to put your opinions in someone else's box, but their box is full. You have to get them to empty their box before they'll even think about adding any of your stuff.

Listening to their opinions has to be genuine. You can't shortcut this by pretending to listen or pretending to care, just so they hurry up and empty out their opinion box so you can get to your arguments. You have to be okay with the possibility that you may never get the opportunity in this conversation to share your opinion. (Remember, play the long game.)

Do you see the importance of this? "Slater, I want to tell them what I think. I don't care what they think." I know, but they won't care what you think, unless you care what they think first.

When they are half-way done emptying their box of opinions, resist the urge to jump in with your opinion. It's too soon. When their box is empty, you'll know.

If you really care about your opinions, you will wait to share them.

"So when can I share my opinion?" There's something you will want to understand before you do...

10. The Where

While you are genuinely asking someone what they think about a given topic, make sure you ask them about their "Where."

Most people know *what* they believe because they've been polishing and perfecting their opinion for a long time. But what is more important is *where* this belief came from in the first place.

Check out this fancy schmancy diagram:

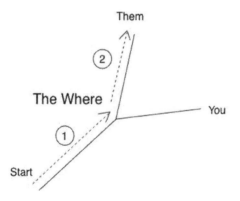

See that fork in the road? That is someone's Where. We all have this place. This is where you and this other person went in different directions. You now want them to come over to where you are. Here's the thing: There is no short-cut.

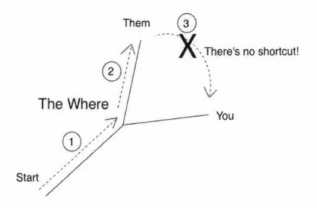

They won't just go from where they are to where you are. They need to *first go back to their Where.*

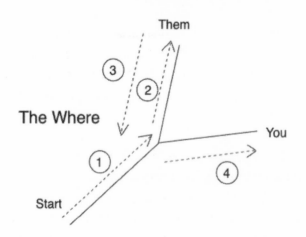

When you ask someone where their opinion came from, you'll get two types of answers:

A simple response such as, "I don't know" or, "I heard it somewhere from someone I think." Something like that.

A dramatic personal story. If you get a dramatic story, just listen. They may get angry or sad retelling their story. That's okay in this context. It is part of the process. Don't even look like you are thinking of something to say back. Once they are done, they will be a new person; more open than ever before.

This is a huge moment either way.

The person with the simple response is realizing that maybe their treasured opinion is not built on as secure a foundation as they thought. This may be the first time they have ever questioned their belief. And now they are questioning it themselves.

The person with the dramatic story feels a huge weight taken off their shoulders, because no one has ever talked to them this deeply before. They will feel heard and validated. People love to feel significant, and if you are genuinely interested in them, they will feel good about themselves, they will like you, and they will be more likely to listen to your opinions.

People often have an opinion because their Where was a bad experience. They may be an atheist because they grew up around hypocritical Christians, or a supporter of single-payer healthcare because they got in a car accident and didn't have health insurance. They may argue against capitalism because their greedy boss laid them off or be anti-gun because a friend of theirs was the victim of an armed robbery. If all we do is share our opinions, we'll never know where someone picked up theirs.

At this point, after realizing they either don't know why they have their opinion, or they feel heard for maybe the first time, the person is usually "freed up" to think about the issue in a fresh way. This is when they will typically ask for your opinion. Now is your time to shine!

But, before we proceed, let's make sure the boxes are checked. Ask yourself:

- Is this conversation one-on-one and in-person?
- Are their defenses down?
- Am I willing to have my mind changed?
- Am I genuinely trying to change someone's mind as opposed to trying to "win"?
- Are all emotions in check?

- Am I willing to play the long game?
- Is their opinion box empty?
- Have I clearly identified the *Where* of their opinion?

All good? Beautiful. *Now* it is time for you to share your opinion! Let's talk about the best way to do that.

11. Moral Foundations

I highly recommend the book The 5 Love Languages by Gary Chapman. It is short and life changing.

Here is how Gary Chapman describes Love Languages:

> My conclusion after thirty years of marriage counseling is that there are basically five emotional love languages—five ways that people speak and understand emotional love. In the field of linguistics, a language may have numerous dialects or variations. Similarly, within the five basic emotional love languages, there are many dialects....The important thing is to speak the love language of your spouse.[21]

The five love languages Chapman identifies are: gift giving, quality time, words of affirmation, acts of service, and physical touch.

The idea is that we each have a way we feel most loved. We assume that our spouse has the *same* love language, so we think the best way to show them love is the way we want to feel loved. The problem is, they may have a different love language.

For instance, my primary love language is "words of affirmation." I like when my wife compliments me and tells me encouraging things.

So I reciprocate. I tell my wife how beautiful and amazing and wonderful she is. But one day, she told me she didn't feel loved. I thought to myself, "*What*! I tell you every day how beautiful and wonderful you are!"

The thing is, words of affirmation is not *her* primary love language. Her love language is "quality time." I then realized that I've been working too much and not investing enough quality time together with her. We weren't talking the same language.

This book is a marriage saver. Read it. Even if you're not married, it will help your other relationships.

I want to talk about the same idea, but instead of *love languages*, they're called Moral Foundations.

- Progressives' moral foundations are Caring and Fairness.

- Conservatives' moral foundations are Respect, Authority and Purity.[22]

Just like love languages, if you are talking to someone with a different moral foundation, you *must* talk in terms that are meaningful to *them*.

For instance, most commentary on environmentalism and climate change is spoken in the "caring" moral foundation: "We need to take care of Mother Earth, save the animals, love the planet, etc." This caring language appeals more to progressives.

If you are a progressive and you want to communicate your concerns for the environment to a conservative, these arguments are not terribly effective (as you might have experienced yourself). And you can't understand why, because it all makes perfect sense to you! Instead, speak more to the "purity" moral foundation: "The clean air is now dirty, the original forests have been destroyed, we need to be good stewards of the planet, etc."

Two professors from Stanford and Berkeley tested this and concluded, "Reframing pro-environmental rhetoric in terms of purity —a moral value resonating primarily among conservatives — largely eliminated the difference between liberals' and conservatives' environmental attitudes."[23]

Personally, I have tried to convince political progressives that all immigrants should learn English. My argument can be summed up with basically, "Because it's America, darn it!" (That is: purity of traditions and culture). If you are conservative and reading this, you read that and probably thought, "Yes, that makes sense." To a fellow conservative, that is a fine argument to make. They will be convinced and they will think I'm great. As a conservative talk radio host, this has always been my job inside the echo chamber.

The thing is, this never convinced anyone who did not already agree with me. Why? Because progressives don't speak that language.

Progressives talk in terms of caring and fairness. So, a better argument to someone with the Caring and Fairness moral foundation would be, "I think immigrants should speak English, because they will be more likely to get a job and less likely to be discriminated against."[24]

I'm still coming to the same conclusion (immigrants should speak English), but I'm just making the argument in a moral foundation "language" that the other person will understand.

You're probably thinking, "But Slater, why should I change my opinion for another person?"

You are not changing your opinion. You are just changing your argument. And you should change your argument because *it's not about you*. "Wining an argument" is about you. Changing someone's mind is about *them*.

It helps if you think of it as an actual language. If you speak German and you're trying to convince a Japanese person of something, you don't talk to them in German. You learn Japanese.

Similarly, it is extremely difficult to convince someone to change their mind if you don't speak their moral foundation.

12. The Costanza Rule

Earlier, I gave five rules for mind changing. Here is the final rule.

Rule 6: Leave on a high note.

George Costanza, Jerry Seinfeld's best friend in the 1990s hit sitcom Seinfeld, decided that whenever he made a funny joke in a group of people, that was the best moment to leave the room. That way, Funny George is the last thing people remember of him.

In your conversation with someone, it's important to know when to stop. Don't miss your exit.

Fight the urge to keep talking until the person has the ultimate epiphany, "Wow, I was wrong. You are so right. Thank you for saving me!"

That won't happen, and something will go awry while you wait for it.

End on a high note, a point of agreement, some common ground. Pay attention to their body language. If there is a moment when the person leans back, looks up into the corner of their brain as if to say, "Hmm, I've never thought of that before," that's a good place to stop. That is the beginning of when they start to question their opinion. End it there. Let them sleep on it.

If you keep talking, like an overcooked steak, you can ruin the entire experience. Leave on friendly terms, with everyone wanting more.

13. Don't Get Disgusted

A 2016 Pew Research Study titled *Partisanship and Political Animosity* found that perspectives of people in opposing political parties are more negative than at any time in the past twenty-five years.[25]

Seventy percent of Democrats said that Republicans are more close-minded than other Americans. A near majority said Republicans were dishonest (42%), immoral (35%), and unintelligent (33%).

Republicans were asked the same questions. Fifty-two percent of Republicans said that Democrats are more close-minded than other Americans. A similar percentage said Democrats are immoral (47%), lazy (46%), dishonest (45%) and unintelligent (32%).

What Republicans and Democrats say about each other

% of Republicans who say Democrats are more____ than other Americans

				About the same
Closed-minded	52%	Open-minded	11%	35%
Immoral	47	Moral	3	49
Lazy	46	Hard-working	3	50
Dishonest	45	Honest	2	52
Unintelligent	32	Intelligent	3	64

% of Democrats who say Republicans are more____ than other Americans

Closed-minded	70%	Open-minded	5%	23%
Dishonest	42	Honest	5	51
Immoral	35	Moral	9	54
Unintelligent	33	Intelligent	7	58
Lazy	18	Hard-working	9	71

Note: Don't know/No answer not shown.
Source: Survey conducted March 2-28 and April 5-May 2, 2016.

PEW RESEARCH CENTER

A vast majority of politically engaged Republicans and Democrats, between 60 and 70%, say the opposing party makes them afraid and angry.

More than these negative characteristics, Pew asked if you believe someone in the other party is a threat to the country. In 1994, about 20% of people thought those on the other side of the aisle were a threat. Today, it's 55%.

John Gottman, PhD, is the author of *The Seven Principles for Making Marriage Work*, and has spent decades studying marriage and relationships. He says the communication style that best predicts the end of a marriage is contempt:

> Sarcasm and cynicism are types of contempt. So are name-calling, eye-rolling, mockery and hostile humor. In whatever form, contempt is poisonous to a relationship because it conveys disgust. It is virtually impossible to resolve a problem when your partner is getting the message you are disgusted with him or her. Inevitably, contempt leads to more conflict, rather than reconciliation.[26]

What is true for marriage is true for all relationships: try not to get disgusted at someone with whom you disagree. When you have contempt for them, you will want nothing to do with them. And they will want nothing to do with you.

You may be thinking, "But Slater, I really do have disgust for this person and what they believe." Okay, but having contempt for someone also makes it impossible for you to ever spread your opinions. So, for the sake of your important cause, whether it's climate change, tax policy or your religious beliefs, let go of your contempt for them.

"Slater, you don't understand. This person is SO WRONG! And their opinion is dangerous. I have to hate them."

In 1988, Oprah had a panel of white supremacists on her show. She said she has never felt such evilness and hatred in all her life. One of those skinheads was Mike Barrett. Twenty-three years later, Mike went back on Oprah's show...to apologize.

A year after the original show, Mike went to prison for defacing a synagogue. The crew they put him on in prison was made up entirely of black men. Imagine Mike, a man who had swastikas tattooed all over his neck and arms (so his opinions were quite obvious), working alongside a group of black men:

> These guys accepted me for who I was. They treated me like a human being. It taught me that everybody is a human being and we can't just hate people.[27]

It was the acceptance from the black men around Mike that made him see how wrong he was. They did not beat him into submission. They did not have contempt for him. And if *they* didn't have contempt for a racist skinhead, surely *we* can overcome contempt for someone with a different opinion, too.

14. Find Common Ground

In addition to hosting a radio show, I have been a pundit on cable TV shows for the last eight years. It may sound exciting. But in reality, these appearances are the most unfulfilling experience in my work. I go to a studio which looks like a broom closet, stare into a camera and get in an argument with someone for two to four minutes. The camera turns off, I take off my ear piece and feel pretty worthless. No one listened to anyone. We just yelled past each other. What was the point of that? We filled time, I suppose, but that's about it.

This is not news. It is news entertainment. By design, no one is there to listen to other perspectives. Everyone is an actor playing a part. It is a pretty big waste of time for everyone involved. But this is what we have all been trained to think debate is: who can yell the loudest and sound the most confident. It's a lie.

Be inspired, instead, by Daryl Davis, a black, blues-playing piano man. That's his job; but his calling is to convert Klan members. How does he do it? He befriends them.

In 1983, Daryl was playing a gig at a truck stop in Frederick Maryland. During a break, a man came up to Daryl, slapped him on the back and said, "I've never seen a black man play the piano like Jerry Lee Lewis!" Daryl responded, "Where do you think Jerry Lee Lewis learned to play the piano? He learned to play that style from black blues and boogie-woogie piano players."

The man didn't believe him, but offered to buy Daryl a drink anyway. As his drink was being poured he said, "You know, this is the first time I've ever had a drink with a black man."

"Really? Why's that?"
"Because I'm a member of the Ku Klux Klan."[28]

Turns out, the man was recently banned from the Klan because he stole money from the group to buy tickets to a Hulk Hogan WrestleMania event. But Daryl used this contact to get in touch with the leader of the Maryland KKK, Roger Kelly. After they met and talked for a few hours, the Klan leader reached out his hand to Daryl and said, "Stay in touch."[29]

Daryl then started inviting the KKK Grand Dragon to his gigs and then to his house:

Sometimes I would invite over some of my Jewish friends, some of my black friends, some of my white friends, just to engage Mr. Kelly in conversation...I didn't want him to think I was some exception. I wanted him to talk to other people. After awhile he began coming [to my house] by himself, no [bodyguard]. He trusted me that much. After a couple years, he became Imperial Wizard - the national leader. He began inviting me to *his* house.

Eventually Roger Kelly quit the Klan.

The three Klan leaders here in Maryland - Roger Kelly, Robert White, and Chester Doles - I became friends with each one of them. When the three Klan leaders left the Klan and became friends of mine, that ended the Ku Klux Klan in the state of Maryland. Today there is no more Ku Klux Klan in the state. They've tried to revive it every now and then, but it immediately falls apart. Groups from neighboring states might come in and hold a rally ... but it's never taken off.

Daryl has convinced over 200 men to leave the KKK. He has a closet in his house full of robes from former Klansmen. This sounds like a great victory, right? But it hasn't come without criticism:

> I had one guy from an NAACP branch chew me up one side and down the other, saying, you know, we've worked hard to get ten steps forward. Here you are sitting down with the enemy having dinner, you're putting us twenty steps back." I pull out my robes and hoods and say, "Look, this is what I've done to put a dent in racism. I've got robes and hoods hanging in my closet by people who've given up that belief because of my conversations sitting down to dinner. They gave it up. How many robes and hoods have you collected?" And then they shut up.

How has Daryl been so successful?

> The most important thing I learned is that when you are actively learning about someone else you are passively teaching them about yourself. So if you have an adversary with an opposing point of view, give that person a platform. Allow them to air that point of view, re-

gardless of how extreme it may be. And believe me, I've heard things so extreme at these rallies they'll cut you to the bone.

Give them a platform.

You challenge them. But you don't challenge them rudely or violently. You do it politely and intelligently. And when you do things that way, chances are they will reciprocate and give you a platform. [The klansmen] and I would sit down and listen to one another over a period of time. And the cement that held his ideas together began to get cracks in it. And then it began to crumble. And then it fell apart.

I don't seek to convert them, but if they spend time with me, they can't hate me. He sees that I want the same thing for my family as he does for his. If you can work on the things in common, that's how you build friendship.[30]

Daryl knows the secret.

Now, so do you.

15. We're Small Enough Now

> Whenever you are about to find fault with
> someone, ask yourself the following question:
> What fault of mine most nearly resembles the
> one I am about to criticize?
>
> –Marcus Aurelius [31]

Jim Collins is the author of *Good to Great: Why Some Companies Make the Leap...And Others Don't.* His twenty-two person research team spent four years trying to determine what made companies grow from merely good organizations to great ones. They focused on the personal characteristics of the CEOs.

Collins describes a Level 4 leader — the second highest — as someone who stimulates his employees to high performance standards and casts a clear and compelling vision for the future. A level 5 leader — the highest level — does the same thing, but adds the most important characteristic of all...humility. Co-workers and employees who wrote about these Level 5 leaders described them as quiet, humble, modest, reserved, shy, gracious, mild-mannered, self-effacing, understated, and "does not believe his own clippings".[32]

Take Darwin E Smith, the twenty year CEO of Kimberly-Clark, maker of Kleenex, Scott paper towels and Huggies. When he was asked what drove him to make his company so successful, he replied, "I was just trying to become qualified for the job."

Ken Iverson was the CEO of Nucor. He took Nucor from the verge of bankruptcy to becoming the largest steel company in America. This is how a board member described Iverson:

> Ken is a very modest and humble man. I've never known a person as successful in doing what he's done that's as modest. And I work for a lot of CEOs of large companies. That's true in his private life as well. The simplicity of him. I mean little things, like he always gets his dogs at the local pound. He has a simple house that he's lived in for ages. He only has a carport and he complained to me one day about how he had to use his credit card to scrape the frost off his windows and he broke the credit card. "You know, Ken, there's a solution for it; enclose your carport." And he said, "Ah, heck, it isn't that big of a deal..." He's that humble and simple.[33]

When Sam Walton, the founder of Wal-Mart, was worth over $100 billion, he drove his 1979 Ford F150 pickup truck. One of the richest men in the world, "I still can't believe it was news that I get my hair cut at the barbershop. Where else would I get it cut? Why do I drive a pickup truck? What am I supposed to haul my dogs around in, a Rolls-Royce?"

But it's not just good for the bottom line. Middle managers who work at companies with humble leaders feel more engaged and committed to their job. They also feel their work is more meaningful and are more motivated to collaborate and share information.

On the other hand, Collins found that "in over two thirds of the comparison cases, we noted the presence of a gargantuan personal ego that contributed to the demise or continued mediocrity of the company".

If humble CEOs lead successful companies and empower their employees, can humble people convince family members, co-workers, friends and even strangers to change their minds? I would argue it's the only way.

How do we stay humble? Perspective.

When NASA released a picture of the Earth from four billion miles away, we were merely a tiny dot amidst rays of light from the sun. Noted astronomer Carl Sagan wrote in *Pale Blue Dot:*

> Look again at that dot. That's here. That's home. That's us. On it everyone you love, everyone you know, everyone you have ever heard of, every human being who ever was, lived out their lives. The aggregate of our joy and suffering, thousands of confident religions, ideologies, and economic doctrines, every hunter and forager, every hero and coward, every creator and destroyer of civilization, every king and peasant, every young couple in love, every mother and father, hopeful child, inventor and explorer, every teacher of morals, every corrupt politician, every 'superstar,' every 'supreme leader,' every saint and sinner in the history of our species lived here– on a mote of dust suspended in a sunbeam…It has been said that astronomy is a humbling and character-building experience. There is perhaps no better demonstration of the folly of human conceits than this distant image of our tiny world. To me, it underscores our responsibility to deal more kindly with one another…[34]

After a night of solving the world's problems at his Sagamore Hill Estate in Long Island, president Teddy Roosevelt and his guests would walk outside and look up at the stars. They would stare at one spot of mist in the northern sky: The Galaxy of Andromeda. This galaxy is as large as our Milky Way, and only one of a hundred million galaxies. It's 750,000 light-years away and consists of one hundred billion suns each larger than our sun. After contemplating in amazement, Roosevelt would look to his friends and say, "Now I think we are small enough. Let's go to bed."[35]

With perspective and humility, let's go change some minds.

I hope this advice is helpful. I would love to hear your experience of where you used this insight to change people's minds. You can E-mail me at SlaterRadio@gmail.com or on www.facebook.com/MikeSlaterShow.

BIBLIOGRAPHY

[1] https://www.ted.com/talks/megan_phelps_roper_i_-grew_up_in_the_westboro_baptist_church_here_s_why_i_left/transcript?language=en

[2] http://www.timesofisrael.com/how-a-former-westboro-baptist-church-spokesperson-overcame-her-hatred-of-jews/

[3] https://www.hillaryclinton.com/feed/how-win-thanksgiving-debate-republicans-tips-hillary-clintons-communications-team/

[4] Ryan Holiday. *Ego Is the Enemy*, p. 73.

[5] Ben Franklin, *The Autobiography of Benjamin Franklin*, p. 163.

[6] http://blog.ted.com/the_healthcare/

[7] Ziva Kunda, *Self-Serving Generation and Evaluation of Causal Theories*, 1987.

[8] Alexander Todorov, *Face Value: The Irresistible Influence of First Impressions*, 28.

[9] https://www.princeton.edu/news/2007/10/22/determine-election-outcomes-study-says-snap-judgments-are-sufficient

[10] Petter Johansson, "Failure to Detect Mismatches Between Intention and Outcome in a Simple Decision Task", 2005.

[11] Daniel Goleman *Emotional Intelligence: Why It Can Matter More Than IQ.*, 2005.

[12] http://www.danielgoleman.info/the-brain-and-emotional-intelligence-an-interview-with-daniel-goleman/

[13] http://www.theblaze.com/news/2014/03/20/11-rules-for-debating-a-leftist-from-ben-shapiro/

[14] http://theoatmeal.com/comics/believe

[15] Thomas Jefferson, *Jefferson: Political Writing.*, p. 254.

[16] https://storycorps.org/podcast/storycorps-499-an-experiment/

[17] McLeod, S. A. (2008). Asch Experiment. Retrieved from www.simplypsychology.org/asch-conformity.html

[18] Robert Greene, *The 33 Strategies of War*, p. 99.

[19] Ibid, p. 100.

[20] Dale Carnegie, *How to Win Friends and Influence People*, p. 83.

[21] http://www.5lovelanguages.com/

[22] There is a lot more to this. Please read *The Righteous Mind: Why Good People are Divided by Politics and Religion* by Jonathan Haidt. He also has a great website with a bunch of resources: http://righteous-mind.com/

[23] https://climateaccess.org/system/files/Feinberg_Moral%20Roots%20of%20Environmental%20Attitudes.pdf

[24] https://www.theatlantic.com/politics/archive/2017/06/working-toward-the-same-ends-for-different-reasons/531666/

[25] http://www.people-press.org/2016/06/22/partisanship-and-political-animosity-in-2016/

[26] John Gottman, *The Seven Principles for Making Marriage Work*.

[27] http://www.huffingtonpost.com/entry/the-evil-episode-that-changed-how-oprah-did-tv-forever_us_58d0615fe4b0ec9d29deb992

[28] https://www.theatlantic.com/politics/archive/2015/03/the-audacity-of-talking-about-race-with-the-klu-klux-klan/388733/

[29] http://loveandradio.org/2014/02/the-silver-dollar/

[30] Listen to Daryl tell his story in this podcast interview, it's incredible: http://loveandradio.org/2014/02/the-silver-dollar/

[31] Marcus Aurelius, *The Emperor's Handbook: A New Translation of the Meditations*, p. 120.

[32] https://hbr.org/2005/07/level-5-leadership-the-triumph-of-humility-and-fierce-resolve

[33] Jim Collins, *Good to Great: Why Some Companies Make the Leap...And Others Don't*, p. 28.

[34] Carl Sagan, *Pale Blue Dot: A Vision of the Human Future in Space*, 1997.

[35] William Beebe, *The Book of Naturalists,* p. 234.

Made in the USA
Las Vegas, NV
13 November 2020